D0916864

First published 1995 © Robert Frederick Ltd.,
Downwood, Claverton Down Road, Bath BA2 6DT

Printed and bound in Singapore

A BOOK OF QUOTATIONS

FOR THE ONE I LOVE

Regatta at Argenteuil by Claude Monet

"We are all born for love; it is the principle of existence and its only end."

Benjamin Disraeli

"He who binds to himself a joy
Does the winged life destroy;
But he who kisses the joy as it flies
Lives in eternity's sunrise."

William Blake

"You will find as you look back upon your life that the moments when you have really lived are the moments when you have done things in the spirit of love."

Henry Drummond

"Who, being loved, is poor?"

Oscar Wilde

"It's a funny thing about life; if you refuse to accept anything but the best, you very often get it."

Somerset Maugham

"Love, all alike, no season knows, nor clime,
Nor hours, age, months, which are the rags of time."

John Donne

"We have no more right to consume happiness without producing it
than to consume wealth without producing it."

George Bernard Shaw

"She will never win him, whose
Words had shown she feared to lose."

Dorothy Parker

"'Tis sweet to know there is an eye will mark
Our coming, and look brighter when we come."

Lord Byron: Don Juan

"Those undeserved joys which come uncalled and make us
more pleased than grateful are they that sing."

Thoreau

The Pont Royal and the
Pavillion de Flores, Paris
by Camille Pissarro

View of L'Estaque
by Paul Cézanne

"He is not laughed at that laughs at himself first."
Thomas Fuller

"Forgive and forget. Sour grapes make for a lousy wine."
Author Unidentified

"We know what happens to people who stay in the middle of the road.
They get run over."
Aneurin Bevan

"For an instant, love can transform the world."
Author Unidentified

"One can know a man from his laugh, and if you like a man's laugh before you
know anything of him, you may confidently say that he is a good man."
Dostoevsky

"Happiness makes up in height for what it lacks in length."
Robert Frost

"There is nothing like staying at home for real comfort."
Jane Austen

"Challenges can be stepping stones or stumbling blocks.
It's just a matter of how you view them."
Author Unidentified

"Loyalty brings its own reward."
Proverbs 11.17

"Cooking is like love. It should be entered into with abandon or not at all."
Harriet van Horne

"Happiness is not the absence of problems;
but the ability to deal with them."
Author Unidentified

"If it were not for hopes, the heart would break."
Thomas Fuller

Dance at Bougival
by Auguste Renoir

The Hôtel des Roches Noires at Trouville
by Claude Monet

"By all means marry; if you have a good wife, you'll become happy;
if you have a bad one, you'll become a philosopher."

Socrates

"It is not love that is blind, but jealousy."

Lawrence Durrell

"Real generosity is doing something nice for someone who'll never find it out."

Frank A. Clark

"All who joy would win
Must share it, –
Happiness was born a Twin."

Lord Byron: Don Juan

"Though jealousy be produced by love, as ashes are by fire,
yet jealousy extinguishes love as ashes smother the flame."

Margaret of Navarre

"Treasure the love you receive above all. It will survive long after
your gold and good health have vanished."

Og Mandino

"As a wife you may be your husband's salvation;
as a husband you may be your wife's salvation."

1 Corinthians 7:16

"Let there be spaces in your togetherness."

Kahlil Gibran

"A kiss can be a comma, a question mark or an exclamation point.
That's basic spelling that every woman ought to know."

Mistinguett

"Lovers may be, and indeed, generally are enemies,
but they can never be friends."

Lord Bryon

Winter, Louveciennes by Alfred Sisley

The Skiff by Auguste Renoir

"A wise man sings his joy in the closet of his heart."
Tibullus

"Well-married, a man is winged – ill-matched, he is shackled."
Henry Ward Beecher

"Perfect love leaves no room for fear."
John, 1st Century

"The chains of marriage are so heavy that it takes
two to bear them, sometimes three."
Alexandre Dumas Fils

"Most people are about as happy as they make up their minds to be."
Abraham Lincoln

"Men always want to be a woman's first love; women have a more
subtle instinct: what they like is to be a man's last romance."
Author Unidentified

"Gratitude is not only the greatest of virtues,
but the parent of all the others."

Cicero

"Nothing is more difficult, and therefore more precious,
than to be able to decide."

Napoleon I

"A man's wife has more power over him than the state has."

Ralph Waldo Emerson

"The most wasted day is that in which we have not laughed."

Chamfort

"Character is like stock in trade; the more of it a man possesses,
the greater his facilities for making additions to it. Character is power –
is influence; it makes friends; creates funds; draws patronage and support;
and opens a sure and easy way to wealth, honour and happiness."

Author Unidentified

The Old Market and the
Rue de L'Epicerie, Rouen,
Morning, Grey Weather
by Camille Pissarro

The Grand Canal, Venice
by Edouard Manet

"Any married man should forget his mistakes –
no use two people remembering the same thing."

Duane Dewel

"Courage is often an effect of fear."

French Proverb

"Everything which is properly business we must keep carefully
separate from life. Business requires earnestness and method:
life must have a freer handling."

Johann Wolfgang von Goethe

"Wives are young men's mistresses, companions for middle age,
and old men's nurses."

Francis Bacon

"One should oblige everyone to the extent of one's ability.
One often needs someone smaller than oneself."

La Fontaine

"Every man is the architect of his own fortune."
Sallust

"Jealousy: that dragon which slays love under the pretence of keeping it alive."
Havelock Ellis

"Courtesy wins woman all as well
As valour may, but he that closes both
Is perfect."
Lord Tennyson

"What is uttered from the heart alone
Will win the hearts of others to your own."
Johann Wolfgang von Goethe

"Marriage, n. the state or condition of a community consisting of a master,
a mistress, and two slaves, making, in all, two."
Ambrose Bierce

Poppies at Argenteuil by Claude Monet

Bonjour Monsieur Gauguin
by Paul Gauguin

"Only two things are necessary to keep one's wife happy. One is to let her think she is having her own way, and the other, to let her have it."
Lyndon B. Johnson

"Our hours in love have wings; in absence crutches."
Colley Cibber

"A happy bridesmaid makes a happy bride."
Lord Tennyson

"Nothing flatters a man as much as the happiness of his wife; he is always proud of himself as the source of it."
Samuel Johnson

"There is never a wrong time to do the right thing."
Author Unidentified

"Marriage is like life in this – that it is a field of battle, and not a bed of roses."
Robert Louis Stevenson

"Nothing is good or bad, but thinking makes it so."
Shakespeare

"Marriage is popular because it combines the maximum of temptation
with the maximum of opportunity."
Shelley

"If you have some respect for people as they are, you can be more
effective in helping them to become better than they are."
John W. Gardner

"This is the secret of joy. We shall no longer strive for our own way;
but commit ourselves, easily and simply, to God's way,
acquiesce in his will and in so doing find our peace."
Evelyn Underhill

"The young man who wants to marry happily should pick out a good mother
and marry one of her daughters – any one will do."
J. Ogden Armour

The Musicians
in the Orchestra
by Edgar Degas

The Luncheon of the Boating Party by Auguste Renoir

"Marriage is three parts love and seven parts forgiveness of sins."

Langdon Mitchell

"One of the best hearing aids a man can have is an attentive wife."

Groucho Marx

"The joys of meeting pay the pangs of absence;
Else who could bear it?"

Nicholas Rowe

"In jealousy there is more of self-love than love."

François de la Rochefoucauld

"There is no more lovely, friendly and charming relationship,
communion or company than a good marriage."

Martin Luther

"Correction does much, but encouragement does more."

Johann Wolfgang von Goethe

"Absence diminishes moderate passions and increases great ones,
as the wind extinguishes tapers and adds fury to fire."
François de la Rochefoucauld

"How great love is, presence best trial makes,
But absence tries how long this love will be."
John Donne

"Gratitude is the heart's memory."
French Proverb

"The fabric of my faithful love
No power shall dim or ravel
Whilst I stay here – but oh, my dear,
If I should ever travel!"
Edna St. Vincent Millay

"I like the dreams of the future better than the history of the past."
Thomas Jefferson

Terrace at Sainte-Adresse
by Claude Monet

Garden of Les Mathurins at Pontoise by Camille Pissarro

"Hold yourself responsible for a higher standard than anyone else expects of you. Never excuse yourself."

Henry Ward Beecher

"Bliss in possession will not last;
Remembered joys are never past."

James Montgomery

"We are all wise for other people, none for himself."

Ralph Waldo Emerson

"Parting is all we know of heaven
And all we need of hell."

Emily Dickinson

"Those marriages generally abound most with love and constancy that are preceded by a long courtship. The passion should strike root and gather strength before marriage be grafted on it."

Joseph Addison

"This swift business
I must uneasy make, lest too light winning
Make the prize light."
Shakespeare: The Tempest

"All life is activity, and joy is the normal accompaniment of that activity."
Ernest von Feuchtersleben

"Of all the passions, jealousy is that which exacts the hardest service
and pays the bitterest wages. Its service is to watch the success of our enemy;
its wages, to be sure of it."
C. C. Colton

"My own business always bores me to death: I prefer other people's."
Oscar Wilde

"Tears may linger at nightfall, but joy comes in the morning."
Psalms 126:5

Flood at Port Marly by Alfred Sisley

Paris, A Rainy Day
by Gustave Caillebotte

"The fountains mingle with the river
And the rivers with the Ocean,
The winds of heaven mix for ever
With a sweet emotion;
Nothing in the world is single;
All things by a law divine
In one spirit meet and mingle,
Why not I with thine?"

Shelley

"It is easier to be wise on behalf on others than to be so for ourselves."

François de la Rochefoucauld

"'Tis better to have loved and lost,
Than never to have loved at all."

Alfred Tennyson

"If love lives on hope, it dies with it; it is a fire which goes out for want of fuel."

Pierre Cornielle

"A kiss, when all is said, what is it?
An oath that's given closer than before;
A promise more precise; the sealing of
Confessions that till then were barely breathed;
A rosy dot placed on the *i* in loving."
Edmond Rostand

"Men are often capable of greater things than they perform. They are sent into
the world with bills of credit, and seldom draw to their full extent."
Author Unidentified

"Come to me in my dreams, and then,
By day I shall be well again,
For then the night will more than pay
The hopeless longing of the day."
Matthew Arnold

"The magic of first love is our ignorance that it can ever end."
Benjamin Disraeli

*Still Life with Glass,
Fruit and Knife
by Paul Cézanne*

On the Seine at Bennecourt
by Claude Monet

"Love doesn't sit there like a stone, it has to be made, like bread;
remade all the time, made new."

Ursula K. le Guin

"Love is a conflict between reflexes and reflections."

Magnus Hirschfield

"A feeling of sadness and longing,
That is not akin to pain,
And resembles sorrow only
As the mist resembles rain."

H. W. Longfellow

"When you tell the truth, you never have to worry about your lousy memory."

Author Unidentified

"All love is sweet,
Given or returned. Common as light is love,
And its familiar voice wearies not ever."

Shelley

"Love is an act of endless forgiveness, a tender look which becomes a habit."
Peter Ustinov

"Love and war are the same thing, and stratagems and policy
are as allowable in the one as the other."
Cervantes

"In love, pain and pleasure are always at war."
Publilius Syrus

"The fruit of the Spirit is love, joy, peace, patience, kindness, goodness,
trustfulness, gentleness and self-control; no law can touch such things as these."
Paul, 1st Century

"Ever has it been that love knows not its own depth
until the hour of separation."
Kahlil Gibran

La Place du Théâtre Français, Paris, Rain by Camille Pissarro

Le Moulin de la Galette
by Auguste Renoir

"Immature love says: 'I love you because I need you.'
Mature love says: 'I need you because I love you.' "

Erich Fromm

"Sometimes when one person is missing, the whole world seems depopulated."

Lamartine

"The man who has never made a fool of himself in love
will never be wise in love."

Theodor Reik

"Love feeds on hope, they say, or love will die – Ah miserie!
Yet my love lives, although no hope have I! – Ah miserie!"

W. S. Gilbert

"Unable are the Loved to die
For Love is Immortality."

Emily Dickinson

"We two form a multitude."
Author Unidentified

"Happiness seems to require a modicum of external prosperity."
Aristotle

"To leave is to die a little;
It is to die to what one loves.
One leaves behind a little of oneself
At any hour, any place."
Edmond Haraucourt

"Marriage is not a finished affair. No matter to what age you live,
love must be continuously consolidated. Being considerate, thoughtful
and respectful without ulterior motives is the key to a successful marriage."
Pamphlet from Chinese Family Planning Centre

"An ideal wife is any woman who has an ideal husband."
Booth Tarkington

Tropical Vegetation,
Martinique
by Paul Gauguin

The Magpie by Claude Monet

"To be patient shows great understanding; quick temper is the height of folly."
Proverbs 14:29

"To know a little of anything gives neither satisfaction nor credit,
but often brings disgrace and ridicule."
Lord Chesterfield

"Married couples who love each other tell each other
a thousand things without talking."
Chinese Proverb

"Modesty gives the maid greater beauty than even the bloom of youth,
it bestows on the wife the dignity of a matron, and reinstates the widow
in her virginity."
Joseph Addison

"Marriage is an empty box.
It remains empty unless you put in more than you take out."
Author Unidentified

"Never has there been one possessed of complete sincerity who did not move others. Never has there been one who had not sincerity who was able to move others."

Mencius

"We learn wisdom from failure much more than success."

Hugh White

"Grow old along with me!
The best is yet to be,
The last of life, for which the first was made:
Our times are in His hand
Who saith 'A whole I planned,
Youth shows but half; trust God: see all nor be afraid!' "

Robert Browning

"Courage is resistance to fear, mastery of fear, not absence of fear."

Mark Twain

Aqueduct and Lock by Paul Cézanne

The Hoar Frost by Camille Pissarro

"Though seas and land betwixt us both
Our faith and troth,
Like separated souls,
All time and space controls:
Above the highest sphere we meet,
Unseen, unknown; and greet as angels greet."

Richard Lovelace

"The Lord watch between me and thee
when we are absent from one another."

Genesis 31:49

"Diligence is the mother of good luck, and God gives all things to industry.
Then plough deep while sluggards sleep, and you shall have
corn to sell and to keep."

Benjamin Franklin

"Our hours in love have wings; in absence crutches."

Colley Cibber

"Like all weak men he laid an exaggerated stress on
not changing one's mind."

Somerset Maugham

"The return makes one love the farewell."

Alfred de Musset

"Security is when I'm very much in love
with somebody extraordinary who loves me back."

Shelley Winters

"We should measure affection, not like youngsters by the ardour of its passion,
but by its strength and constancy."

Cicero

"The love we give away is the only love we keep."

Elbert Hubbard

"An optimist sees an opportunity in every calamity: a pessimist
sees a calamity in every opportunity."

Author Unidentified

Horses on the Course
at Longchamp
by Edgar Degas

The Quay at Bougival
by Berthe Morisot

"God is love, and whoever lives in love lives in union with God,
and God lives in union with him."

John, 1st Century

"Good nature is worth more than knowledge, more than money,
more than honour, to the persons who possess it."

Henry Ward Beecher

"No legacy is so rich as honesty."

Shakespeare: All's Well That Ends Well

"'Lord, how often am I to forgive my brother if he goes on wronging me?
As often as seven times?' Jesus replied, 'I do not say seven times;
I say seventy times seven'."

Matthew 18:21-22

"The ineffable joy of forgiving and being forgiven forms an ecstasy
that might well arouse the envy of the gods."

Elbert Hubbard

"Love is, above all, the gift of oneself."

Jean Anouilh

"Often the difference between a successful marriage and a mediocre one
consists of leaving about three or four things a day unsaid."

Harlan Miller

"One word
Frees us of all the weight and pain of life:
That word is love."

Sophocles

"Have patience with all things, but chiefly have patience with yourself.
Do not lose courage in considering your own imperfections,
but instantly set about remedying them – every day begin the task anew."

Ascribed to St. Francis de Sales

"Absence sharpens love; presence strengthens it."

Thomas Fuller

The Artist's Garden, Irises
by Claude Monet